Susan McLeod

SEASONS
OF LIFE

Susan McLeod

SEASONS OF LIFE

atmosphere press

TABLE OF CONTENTS

Part 3 Seasons of Life

Part 4 Holidays

PART 1

Childhood

Birthday Cake

My Mother made each child a birthday cake
Homemade and into the oven to bake
Each child chose the flavor of their cake
And their favorite icing she did make
Blow out the candles and make a wish
Eat slices of cake and ice cream in a dish

Birthday Wishes

A birthday only comes once a year
Everyone offers good wishes and cheers
Hope you have a happy birthday today
And wish you many more to come your way
Before you know it, your next birthday is here
Birthdays always seem to come faster every year

Black and White TV

The black and white TV was in our den
There were no remotes back then
We watched the news in black and white
The whole family, every night

Bubble Bath

Into the bubble bath I would go
Covered in bubbles, including my toes
Big bubbles raising up in the air
Bubbles, bubbles everywhere
Bubble baths a favorite of mine
Bubble baths are wonderful any time

Tooth Fairy

When outside to play
I lost a front tooth today
That night I went to bed
Thoughts of the tooth fairy in my head
She did come during the night
And left something shiny and bright
Eight quarters staring at me
I was so happy as can be

Ball

Back and forth I toss my ball
Against the school brick wall
The last toss the ball went over the wall
Now I need to stop to find my ball

Baseball

Baseball was my favorite game
I even played in the rain
With my catcher's glove, ball and bat
And my baseball team hat
I do remember those baseball days
With happy memories to this day

Fishing

I liked fishing on any day
Even when it was a rainy day
In the boat or standing at the dock
Or going to the river lock
With my pole and tackle box
Along with my lunch box

Hoops

Roll, roll our hoops on the grass they go
Which way they fall, we don't know
Playing with our hoops was lots of fun
Kept my friends and I on the run
I remember a simpler time
When playing hoops was very fine

Kaleidoscope

A special birthday gift to me
A kaleidoscope to play and see
Patterns, colors changing all the time
So happy this birthday present is mine
The kaleidoscope on a very cold day
So much fun when you could not go out to play

Baby Doll

My Baby doll was special to me
She had long brown hair like me
My Mother made matching dresses for us to wear
I took her to church and everywhere
I had a nice baby carriage to wheel her around
And wheeled her all around my town

Paper Dolls

It was fun playing with paper dolls on rainy days
When we could not go out to play on summer days
Also playing with paper dolls on chilly fall days
And in the wintertime on cold snowed in days
We had fun cutting out the paper doll clothes
And dressing and placing in different poses
We gave each paper doll a name
Playing with paper dolls an inside game

Doll House

My doll house was very pretty to see
It was the color of pink sweet peas
I played with my doll house on a rainy day
When I could not go outside to play
Memories of my doll house never fade away
Even to this very day

Hopscotch

Playing hopscotch, a lot of fun
And very nice when I won
My friends and I skipped and hopped
We never played when it was very hot
Many various locations would do
Sidewalks, playgrounds and driveways to name a few
Now my granddaughter plays hopscotch today
Brings back memories of my yesterdays

Jump Rope

Jump rope games so much fun to do
During spring, summer and fall too
My friends and I, outside on the sidewalk
All of us concentrating with no talk
Taking turns with jumping and keeping score
My friends and I were never bored

Back to School

I recall my summer days very well
Being happy not to hear the school bell
The summer days went by so fast
I would have liked them to last and last
Soon the summer days will go away
Then back to school with no more summer play

Walking to School

Walking to school on a sunny day
I want to stop and play
It's so nice outside
I don't want to be inside
Now I need to wait till the school day ends
Then I can play outside with my friends

School Vacation

Summer vacation is a lot of fun
When you can be out in the sun
Being outdoors every day
Having lots of time to play
Going back to school seems so far away
Summer please don't go away

High School Graduation

Graduation day has finally come
The required schoolwork is done
The night before it was hard to sleep
Even when I tried counting sheep
Graduation excitement in the air
Family and friends are every where
After graduation a party for me
To celebrate with my friends and family

PART 2

Family

Photo Albums

My photo albums hold many photos dear to me
Many are black and white, along with color ones to see
Birthdays, anniversaries and graduations to name a few
Photos of vacations, weddings and holidays too
Looking at the photo albums from time to time
Brings back happy memories of mine

Reunion

Every year a very large family affair
All the family came together at the fair
We spend the day visiting and having fun
On the rides, playing games, and tasting pies with everyone
The family reunion at the fair a lot of fun
Everyone always looked forward to the next one

Baseball Game

Going to a baseball game with my father was fun
Watching the Brooklyn Dodgers in the afternoon sun
At the stadium excitement was all around
I liked watching the pitcher on the mound
The Brooklyn Dodgers were my favorite team
I fantasized I played for then in a dream
Father and I enjoyed watching them play
I would like to be a baseball pitcher some day

Haying

I looked forward to spending the time
Haying with my father in the late summertime
Something I thought was keen
Driving the big mowing machine
Cutting, drying, raking and drying the hay
Then baling and into the barn for use on winter days

Ice Fishing

In the wintertime with my father ice fishing was fun
We find a spot and feel the warm winter sun
Making a hole using the angler in the ice
Catching lots of fish will be nice
I bait and slowly drop my fishing line
To try and catch a fish on the line
My Father and I both wish
We will catch lots of fish

Kite Flying

Kite flying with my father was fun to do
On a Saturday afternoon, just as two
Especially on a windy day
The kites flew up and away
Floating in the blue sky
The two kites go very high

Tree House

My Father built a tree house for me
In a very large old maple tree
A surprise for my birthday for me
I always wanted one in the old maple tree
I played in my tree house every day
Until the summer sun went away
Sometimes on a warm summer night
I would look at the stars that were bright

Chocolate Pudding

Chocolate pudding is good to eat
My Mother made it for a delicious treat
She used whole milk and real chocolate too
Pudding from a box, she said would not do
I can eat chocolate pudding any time
As a snack or dessert after dinner time

Cupcakes

Mother and I put our aprons on
Then a step stool for me to stand on
In the bowl I mix the batter
Careful pouring and try not to splatter
Bake the cupcakes for twelve minutes long
Out they come nice and warm
Let the cupcakes cool a little while
Add vanilla icing and gumdrops for a smile

Knitting

My Mother taught me how to knit
In two chairs side by side, we'd sit
Making a scarf was the first lesson for me
And the yarn was a pretty color to see
The second lesson knitting mittens was fun to do
In my favorite color of light blue
Even to this day I still like my knitting
Because now I do more sitting

Polka Dot Dress

My Mother made the dress for me
Pink and white dots for all to see
Anything pink was a favorite color of mine
I wore something pink most of the time
I loved that dress very much
It had my mother's special touch
When I see pink and white dots, takes me back in time
That dress was always a favorite of mine

Soup

My Mother made soup on a cold day
Each one was delicious in its own way
Hot soup on a winter day
Takes the cold chills away
I have her soup recipes today
Brings back memories of yesterday

Fireplace Mantle

My Grandfather used wood from an old oak tree
The wood was very beautiful to see
Cutting, sanding, and varnishing the wood too
The wood displayed a nice hue
He hung the mantle with care
Above a picture of a black bear

Fishing Pole

My first fishing pole, Grandfather gave to me
It was a birthday present you see
In the summertime we went fishing every Saturday
In his motorboat out on Chesapeake Bay
I learned how to bait the hook and cast out
When I caught a fish, I gave out a shout
I had fun fishing with him on Saturday's
He was wonderful in all kinds of ways

Maple Syrup

Making maple syrup with Grandfather and me
Kept me very busy as a honeybee
Tapping the sugar maples one at a time
The buckets were in a long line
Out in the fresh air and February sun
Watching the maple sap start to run
Collecting the sap and boiling it down
Grandfather's maple syrup was the best around

Stars

Grandfather and I liked to gaze at the stars at night
Lots of the stars shining with bright light
Sharing the telescope to look at the sky
The telescope always helped our eyes
Grandfather was an astronomer professor you see
And he shared his knowledge of the stars with me

Walking

Walking with my grandfather in the fall was neat
With the leaves crunching under our feet
Up we climbed to the very top
At the ridge we would stop
All the fall leaves beautiful to see
Red, orange and yellow the trees
We stand a minute or two
To admire the view

Beauty Parlor

Grandmother takes a seat in the swivel chair
Every six weeks a trim of her hair
Sometimes she'd take me on a day off from school
Which I thought was very cool
I would sit in another swivel chair and spin
While I watched her hair getting a trim

Bingo

My Grandmother said bingo was fun to play
With her girlfriends on any given day
It also was a time to socialize
And she always liked to win a prize
Seventy-five numbers are called
The last game is called cover all

China Cabinet

Grandmother's china cabinet was pretty to see
Many years later she gave the cabinet to me
This beautiful family heirloom
Now inside my dining room
It displays my china, crystal and silverware
I cherish the cabinet with tender loving care

Farm

Going to Grandmother's farm in the summertime
I always had a very nice time
To be out in the fresh air
Seeing farm animals everywhere
Summertime I left my city life
To experience the country life

Rolling Pin

I inherited my grandmother's pie crust rolling pin
She said your pie crust cannot be too thick or thin
That perfect pie crust can be challenging to make
The reward is a pie crust that is golden baked
Having her rolling pin means the world to me
And I am so grateful she gave it to me

Campfire

My friends and I enjoy a campfire on a cool night
Hoping the mosquitoes don't come out to bite
Passing the bag of marshmallows all around
We toast then until they are nice and brown
Telling campfire stories are lots of fun
Everyone had a chance to tell one

Camping

At the campground
The perfect place is found
We set up the tents
And smell the pine scents
Next collect the firewood
Our campfire will be good
Unpack everything
Listening to the birds sing
We fish, swim, canoe, and take hikes
All the kids ride their bikes
On our last day
We pack all the camp stuff away
Say goodbye to everyone
The camping trip was lots of fun

Barbeque

A family barbeque in the summertime
And everyone has a great time
Large bowls of potato, macaroni salad and coleslaw too
With grilling different meats on the barbeque
Ribs, chicken, hamburgers and hotdogs to name a few
Along with baked beans and potato chips too
And ice-cold tea with slices of lemon
For dessert large slices of watermelon

Clambake

We bring everything to the beach
And collect seaweed within our reach
Place large stones in a fire pit
And open-up our beach chairs to sit
When the fire becomes very hot
Make layers of seaweed with the food on top
Let the food steam until it is time to eat
We all agree a clambake at the beach is neat

Diner

For a nice lunch treat
We go to the diner to eat
Everyone is so nice to us
They always make a fuss
We order two of the specials of the day
Homemade soup and sandwiches will come our way
For my dessert I have a slice of apple pie
It's delicious and I happily sigh
My husband has a slice of lemon cake
Which he very quickly ate
Now it is time to go
We will be back soon, I know

Picnic

To go on a picnic down by the lake
Our wicker picnic basket we take
A large blanket spread on the ground
For everyone to sit around
Everything is delicious to eat
Including the brownies for a chocolate treat
We all agree the picnic has been fun
And soon plan to have another one

Beach

I smell the salt in the air
And feel the sea breeze blowing my hair
The beach is very relaxing to me
Lots of beach activity to see
Children making sandcastles by the shore
As I am watching the waves come ashore
Seeing the children on floats
And the many sailboats
I sit on the sandy beach
With the cool water in reach
When I become hot, just jump in
And take a nice long swim
The beach is perfect on any day
Especially on a hot summer day

Cape Cod Bay

I spend the entire day
At a scenic Cape Cod Bay
Many seagulls flying in the air
Children playing on the beach everywhere
I feel the soft sand beneath my feet
The waves going in and out to their own beat
Swimming, sailing, and sunbathing too
A great day at the beach with me and you

Drive-in Movies

On a warm summertime night
Drive-in movies were a delight
We did not have to drive far
In our large family car
Father made sure the windshield was clean
So that the movie could be seen
Drive-in movies a part of my childhood
Watching famous actors from Hollywood
The memories stored in my mind
From another place in time

Fair

Our family enjoyed going to the State fair
We were outside all day in the fresh air
Eating cotton candy and popcorn too
Lots of things to see and do
Seeing the animals and going on the rides
Tasting and judging slices of different pies
So much fun at the State fair
Every year a family affair

Post Office

In the post office waiting in line
I wonder why it is taking so much time
I have lots of packages and questions too
What's a person (like me) in a hurry to do
I wait patiently for my turn to come
I wonder when the person ahead of me will be done
As my mind wanders, I suddenly hear
It's your turn, please come up here

The Park

My friends and I liked to go to the park
We always stayed, just before dark
There's lots of activities to hear, see and do
Swinging on the swings and swimming in the pool too
Hearing the birds singing in the trees
Seeing the flower beds with honeybees
Nice park trails for walking around
Chipmunks scurrying on the ground
Summer days off from school the park was the place to be
Many happy memories my friends and I would agree

Washington, D.C.

Visiting Washington, D.C.
There is so much to see
I spent a whole week there
With things to do everywhere
A wish I was able to finally fulfill
A tour or the White House what a thrill
Beautiful monuments to see all around
With famous National Museums to visit abound
Yes, Washington, D.C. a very special place in the USA
Everyone should plan to visit some day

PART 3

Seasons of Life

Introduction to the Four Seasons

The four seasons come and go
Summer the grass to mow
Fall color leaves that show
Winter it's shovel snow
Spring seeds to sow
The four seasons come and go
I enjoy each one I know

Four Seasons of the Brook

In the Spring the brook is icy cold
See how fast the water goes
Place your feet in the brook on a hot summer day
And let all your cares just float away
Autumn leaves from the trees
Fall into the brook on a gentle breeze
The brook still slowly flows in the Wintertime
It will start to flow fast again in the Springtime

Four Seasons of the Lake

A boat ride on the lake in the Summertime
With fresh air and lots of sunshine
A boat ride on the lake, the season of fall
Cooler temperatures and hear the geese call
In the Wintertime quiet and white with snow
The boat in storage as the snow blows
A boat ride on the lake in the Springtime
With a Spring breeze in the air that feels so fine

Four Seasons of the Oak Tree

Summer the tree offers shade
To sit under and drink a lemonade
Fall the leaves fall to the ground
I rake them up to form a mound
Winter a large bird feeder in the tree
Lots of birds at the feeder are eating I see
Spring new buds on the leaves start to appear
Which indicates Spring is almost here

Sunday Morning

A new day is dawning
It's Sunday morning
Church bells are ringing
Church choirs are singing
In church taking time to reflect and pray
This is the Lord's Day

Sunday Morning Pancakes

Sunday morning breakfast a special treat
Mother's blueberry pancakes so good to eat
I mix the blueberries in the pancake batter
Being very careful not to splatter
Mother pours the batter onto the griddle
I sit down in my chair and try not to fiddle
The pancakes are now ready to eat
This Sunday morning special treat

Sunday Dress

My favorite color was blue
Any shade of blue would do
My Mother made my blue velvet dress
Which I wore as my Sunday best
With matching shoes and a hat of blue
Both went with my blue velvet dress too

Sunday Suit

The color of my suit a light gray
Which I wore to church every Sunday
This suit was my Sunday best
That also had a matching vest
After church the suit was put away
Before I could go out to play

Sunday Church Service

In the church it is quiet and still
Sunlight appears on the windowsills
The stain glass windows are pretty to see
All the different colors appear before me
Everybody is starting to come in
Soon the church service will begin

Sunday Singing

The organ stood grand and tall
Above the Church's front hall
A beautiful instrument for all to see
The wood was made from an oak tree
The pipes were a shiny metal too
That had a unique silver hue
The organist played the organ with care
As the choir's singing filled the air

Dancing

Dancing every Saturday night
My sweetheart held me so tight
The band began to play
We started dancing right away
Dancing all night long
Almost till the early dawn
Now it is time to go home to bed
I will have pleasant dreams in my head

Wedding Band

My wedding band reminds me of a happy time
Those memories go way back in my mind
I remember like it was yesterday
Our day was wonderful in every way
As we started our life together
We agreed it would be forever
I close my eyes and can see that day
It was a picture-perfect day

Introduction to Fall

Fall is a beautiful time of the year
The air is crisp and clear
The color of the leaves on the trees
Oranges, yellows and reds to see
Lots of raking must be done
Before the setting of the fall sun
The air temperature a lot cooler too
Mums with orange, yellow and red hues
Apple cider and apples to drink and eat
Two of fall's delicious treats

Apple Picking

In the apple orchard today
To pick apples on a fall day
Bright sunshine and fresh air
And apples everywhere
The smell of fresh apples on the trees
A nice healthy snack for you and me
Delicious apple pies to bake
Homemade applesauce to make

Apple Cider Doughnuts

Apple cider doughnuts in the fall
Memories that I can recall
I remember from my childhood
Apple cider doughnuts that smelled so good
Doughnuts plain or lightly sugared to eat
With breakfast or as an in-between treat

Apple Pie

I use my mother's recipe for an apple pie
Her favorite apples were the Northern Spys
In the kitchen freshly cut apples fill the air
I make and roll out my pie crust with care
Set the oven knob timer to pre-bake
Then the pie goes into the oven to bake
The pie comes out golden brown
I place the pie on a cooling rack to set down
Apple pie goes good with vanilla ice cream
And/or fresh homemade whipped cream

Applesauce

Every fall our mother made applesauce as a special treat
Her homemade applesauce was so good to eat
Peel, core, and slice the apples and place in the pot
Then add cinnamon, sugar and a little water to the lot
Apples cooking with cinnamon and sugar fill the air
Delicious apple smells are everywhere
Another reason fall is a favorite season of mine
I still make homemade applesauce which takes me back in time

Bittersweet
Picking bittersweet in the fall
To place in a vase in my front hall
Climbing up a ladder in the tree
In the tree, colors of orange I see
Being careful to cut some down
Let it gently fall to the ground
Take the bittersweet home with me
Next year I will come back to the same tree

Walking through the Woods
Walking through the woods in the fall a place to be
Enjoying the colors of the leaves on the trees to see
Everything around me is so peaceful and quiet too
The fall sky with white clouds and a shade of blue
Squirrels, chipmunks and birds with my walk I see
Acorns and pretty leaves dropping from the trees
When the sunlight starts to slowly fade away
Time to go home and come back another day

Woodcutting
Outside in the late fall air
All the trees are now bare
I need to cut wood for the wintertime
Lucky for me today, there is sunshine
I cut lots of wood today
Tomorrow will haul it away
Into the shed the wood will go
I make sure I have enough before the snow

Introduction to Winter
Outside in the icy air
Winter is everywhere
Tasting snowflakes on my tongue
Drinking hot chocolate is a lot of fun
Dripping icicles in the air
Hanging from the roof with care
Hot dog roasts in the wintertime
Out in the snowy woods is fine
On a cold winter day outside
I like sitting by a cozy fire inside

Hot Cocoa

A mug of hot cocoa on a cold day
Chase's the winter's chills away
With fresh cookies that I have baked
Hot cocoa delicious to make
Warm the milk in a saucepan
Add the cocoa from the tin can
Stir and add some marshmallows in a mug
It's like receiving a nice warm hug

Hot Dog Roast

We bring a large thermos with baked beans to eat
And mustard, sauerkraut, rolls and hot dog meat
In the woods on snowshoes to find the perfect spot
We start a fire which becomes nice and hot
The hot dogs and beans go together for a great hot dog roast
Followed by making s'mores with marshmallows to toast

Sledding

Sledding after a large snowstorm is fun to do
With all my friends and siblings too
It's cold outside but we do not care
A frosty chill in the winter air
We climb up the big hill with our sleds in tow
Then on our sleds and down the hill we go
All afternoon having so much fun
We come in when there is no more winter sun

Sleigh Ride

I remember my very first sleigh ride
Grandmother and Grandfather at my side
Three feet of new white snow
And into the sleigh and off we go
In the sleigh my grandmother holds my hand
Grandfather keeps the horses in his command
Going up and down the snowy hillsides
A sleigh ride through the countryside

Snow Angel

Last night's snowstorm brought lots of snow
In my snow suit, boots, hat, and mittens out I go
Perfect for making a snow angel in the snow
I lay down and move my arms and legs to and fro
Carefully I stand up in the snow
And see my beautiful angel below

Snowflakes

Snowflakes, snowflakes everywhere
Falling through the cold, cold air
Stick out your tongue to taste one
Tasting snowflakes lots of fun
No two snowflakes are alike
Snowflakes are a winter's delight

Snowman

Outside it's cold with lots of snow
I put on my winter clothes and out I go
Roll the snow into three different sized balls
My snowman will be five feet tall
Then make the mouth and eyes with pieces of coal
Add a scarf and hat so he does not get cold
A bright orange carrot for a nose
My snowman has a striking pose
I hope he won't melt too soon
When the sun is warm in the afternoon

Introduction to Spring

Each year I look forward to Spring
To see what it will bring
How many more days till Spring
When the birds start to sing
Then Spring is finally here
Flowers blooming everywhere
Tulips, hyacinth, and daffodils are blooming
Lots of Spring yard cleanup's looming
Spring a changing time
Before the Summertime

The Birds

One of the best parts of Spring
Is to hear all the different birds sing
They start to sing just before dawn
And wake me and I yawn
Melodies drift through the air
In my bed I listen with care
In harmony the birds all sing
Welcoming a new day of Spring

Cherry Blossoms

Every Springtime in Washington, D.C.
I look forward to a visit with you and me
The cherry blossoms are a pretty sight
With the colors of pinks in the sunlight
The blossoms are dainty and hang from the trees
The blow slowly and gently in the breeze
The pink cherry blossoms of Spring in bloom
The blossoms always go away too soon

Spring Cleaning

Once a year it was Spring cleaning day
Mother always cleaned on a warm sunny day
From top to bottom, we cleaned all day
There was no time for outdoor play
Washing all the glass windows with care
We rinse and let them dry in the air
Curtains, drapes, and rugs too
The oak floors were buffed to their original hue
When all the Spring cleaning was done
It would be three seasons before the next one

Forsythia

A sure sign of Spring is when the Forsythia bloom
That which chase's away the Winter's gloom
Sometimes called the Easter tree
Blooms around Easter time you see
You can force the blooms inside
And not wait till they bloom outside
Forsythia a yellow color such a delight
Like bright splashes of sunlight

Lilacs

Every Spring my lilacs bloom
I place some in a vase in my living room
Shades of different purples everywhere
Fragrant scents fill the air
They only bloom for two weeks every year
And offer some Springtime cheer
Memories of my lilacs bring me back in time
Still today a favorite flower of mine

Lily of the Valley

When the lily of the valley first appears
Indicates that Springtime is very near
Lily of the valley likes a shady spot
Out of the bright sun which is too hot
Six white tepals form a shape of a bell
The flowers have a light fragrance smell
A favorite of brides with their wedding day
The flowers are said to bring luck their way

Spring Rain

A pretty rainbow appears in the sky
The seven colors are pleasing to the eye
After a Spring rain the cool air comes in
The rain barrels hold the water within
After a gentle Spring rain, I can tell
The outside air has a fresh clean smell
Water droplets on the flowers sparkle in the sun
Children splashing in mud puddles oh what fun
Being careful not to get the mud in their eyes
The children like to make lots of mud pies

Introduction to Summer

How I love the Summertime
Warm weather and a blue skyline
Spending long periods of time outdoors
And Summer vacations at the seashores
Watching the flowers and vegetables grow
And every week the grass lawns to mow
Swimming, playing and working out in the sun
Watermelon, BBQ's and the beach are fun
Eating lots of ice cream on a hot summer day
Just letting the summer days idle away

Farm Stand

I go to the farm stand twice a week
To buy fresh vegetables to eat
Sweet corn a favorite of mine
Yellow and green beans are divine
Lettuce, tomatoes, and cucumbers you can't beat
And tasty radishes with some dark red beets
Spinach, peppers and broccoli are good to eat
Farm fresh vegetables a Summertime treat
Fresh berries in season a beautiful sight
And zucchini a late Summertime delight

Hammock

I remember my hammock and me
In between two big oak trees
Swinging in the cool shade
Sipping an ice-cold lemonade
Feel the warmth of the sun and the breeze
Makes me sleepy and I feel at ease
I close my eyes and listen to the birds sing
The different sounds form a harmonious ring

Porch Swinging

On the porch swing back and forth I go
Pushing with my feet to and fro
Hearing the birds singing in the trees
Surrounded by the Summertime breeze
In the porch swing during nighttime
Looking at the bright stars that shine
Listening to the crickets sounds near by
The full moon shining in the night sky
Memories come back to me
Just the porch swing and me

Summer Day

Above me a summer sky and a blue color that catches my eye
The warm summer sunshine, shinning on me feels so fine
Lying on the grass on a warm summer day
I watch the white puffy clouds come my way
Making animals from the shapes of the clouds
I say the name of each one out loud
Still gazing at the clouds that come my way
It's a great way to spend a perfect summer day

Swimming Hole

It's off to the swimming hole I go
With my friends and siblings in tow
Especially on a hot summer day
When it's way too hot to play
The swimming hole the place to be
Lots of water splashing you will see
Swinging from a rope and cold water to jump in
Everyone had large truck tire tubes to float in
Swimming in the cold water refreshing on a hot day
The swimming hole childhood memories of yesterdays

Swimming Pool

Swimming in the City Park pool
The water was so nice and cool
When it was a very hot day
Lots of water fun and play
Taking turns with the diving board for all to see
With all my swimming friends and me
Swimming lessons were important to
To make sure everyone could do
The City Park pool a wonderful time
In the long, beautiful days of Summertime

Trees

The trees in the Summertime and a tire rope swing under a tree
Offer shade from the sunshine and lots of fun for you and me
Reading a book under a tree and a time to spend outside the house
Trees are great for playing in a Summertime tree house
Lying in a hammock between two large trees
And feeling a nice gentle summer breeze

PART 4

Holidays

Introduction to the Holidays

The holidays are a lot of fun
Keeps us all busy and on the run
The holidays come and go by so fast
I wish they would just last and last

Halloween

Halloween is a fun time for all
Witches and ghosts are having a ball
Jack-o-lanterns make a pretty sight
When they can be lite by candlelight
Children to plan what costumes to wear
Trick or treating if you only dare
Trick or treating for children is fun to do
With lots of Halloween parties too
Knocks at the door, who can it be
It's the children in costumes, I see
I hand out the candy to each one
The children are having so much fun

Veterans Day

Every November eleventh is Veterans Day
Our Veterans kept us from harm's way
In our history a very important date
The service of Veterans we celebrate
To all the Veterans we are grateful to you
For your Military service and dedication too
Our Veterans the Navy, Army, and Marine Corps too
Along with the Coast Guard and the Air Force that flew
To the Veterans of War and Military we applaud you
All the Military branches in peace time and war too

Thanksgiving

Thanksgiving is a thankful time for me
Surrounded by my friends and family
The family is sitting in the living room to see
The Macy's Thanksgiving Day Parade on TV
Then in late afternoon the Thanksgiving table is set
The family sits down, and we all take time to reflect
What we are grateful on this day
To give thanks today and everyday

Christmas

Memories to share with me and you
Decorating the tree and the house too
The Christmas tree has pretty lights
Which are shinning very bright
Delicious Christmas cookies to bake
And special presents to make
Presents to wrap for under the tree
Green and red colorful bows for all to see
A new fresh snow on Christmas Day
The children excited for outdoor play
Going to church on Christmas Day
Spending time with family far away

Christmas Candles in Church

Christmas candles in church are dear to me
Christmas candles such a pretty sight to see
Sitting in the church pews the candles can be seen
On the altar with red and white poinsettias in between
Christmas candles in church have a special light
Christmas candles are such a delight

Christmas Cookies

Making sugar Christmas cookies is fun to do
Lots of stars, angels, and Christmas trees too
Santa Clauses, Christmas wreaths and bells
From the oven comes lots of nice smells
Pack the cookies in Christmas tins
Christmas presents for our kin

Christmas Wreath

Decorating a Christmas wreath was fun to do
With using the colors of silver and blue
The fresh smell of green pine in the air
I place the ornaments on the wreath with care
Then finish with a large bow I add
A silver and blue pattern of plaid
Hang on my front door for all to see
The wreath decorated by me

Santa Claus

I can hardly wait for Santa Claus to come
Each day seems longer than the last one
I hope Santa Claus has good weather to fly his sled
While I am asleep in my nice warm bed
The next morning down to the Christmas tree I run
I can't wait to open all my presents, oh what fun

Kwanzaa

Kwanzaa a happy celebration held once a year
To give thanks to our African ancestors we hold dear
With exchanging special Kwanzaa cards during the week
Listening to music with drums is neat
The kinara with red, green, and black candles aglow
Sharing the unity cup and receiving gifts with bows
The greeting for Kwanzaa, how are you?
Reviewing and practicing the seven principles too
The holiday Kwanzaa means first fruits of the harvest
To celebrate our African heritage at its best

New Year's Day

New Year's Day is here at last
The past year flew by very fast
To reflect on the past year
Especially what I hold dear
Resolutions are fun to make
But very, very easy to break
What resolutions will I make this year?
Or will they start to eventually disappear
I hope the New Year will be good to everyone
Before you know it, another year will be done

Martin Luther King Junior Day

Every year in January, the third Monday
We celebrate Martin Luther King Junior Day
This day to remember what he stood for
All his principles and deeds he fought for
The message for us all, his I have a Dream Speech
At the Lincoln Memorial he did preach
Nineteen sixty- four the Nobel Peace Prize
Faith, hope, forgiveness, love he emphasized
His striking monument is at the National Mall
To remind us, his contributions to us all

Valentine's Day

Valentine's Day is a very romantic day
Hearts, flowers, and chocolates come my way
On my card are pink and red hearts
From my wonderful sweetheart
A beautiful bouquet from my valentine
Pretty yellow roses, a favorite of mine
In a special heart shaped box, I see
An assortment of chocolates for me
Candles on the table give off a soft light
A romantic dinner by candlelight
Spending the day with my sweetheart
Valentine's Day is a day of the heart

Saint Patrick's Day

The Irish is celebrated on Saint Patrick's Day
With green decorations on display
Attending a Saint Patrick's Day parade
Listening to Irish music being played
Corned beef and cabbage to eat
A special Saint Patrick's Day treat
Drinking and enjoying a pint of beer
Raising a glass to an Irish cheer
The green color to wear on this day
Is thought to keep the leprechauns away

Easter

I look forward to Easter every year
Easter is when Springtime is near
An Easter egg hunt is lots of fun
Will I be able to find the last one?
Jellybeans, a chocolate bunny and colored eggs too
Yellow marshmallow chicks and chocolate eggs will do
Mother says do not eat everything up in one day
When everything is gone, put the basket away

Mother's Day

This day comes in the month of May
For the celebration of Mother's Day
Celebrating all the mother's everywhere
With many loving thoughts with care
Some gifts that come their way
Cards and pretty flower bouquets
And special Mother's Day mugs
And lots and lots of heartfelt hugs
Giving Mother's the day off, a nice touch
To tell her that she is appreciated so much
Recognize and honor all the mother's this day
Each of us in our unique and special way

Memorial Day

Memorial Day is an important day in May
Which is also known as Decoration Day
In the morning with other volunteers, I go
We place flags on military graves of long-ago
Attending a Memorial Day parade
Seeing the Rolling Thunder Motorcade
Visiting the War Memorial in the town square
To remember everyone in our hearts with care
This day to reflect on those who gave their lives
Ensuring freedom rights for the World to survive

Flag Day

Flag Day is special to me
I hang my flag outside for all to see
To see the flag fly so high
Fills my heart with pride
A Flag Day parade is special too
To honor the red, white and blue
Everyone celebrates the flag today
The proud flag of the USA

Father's Day

The month of June is Father's Day
Celebrated on the third Sunday
Recognizing fathers and father figures everywhere
We thank them all for their help and care
Fathers have helped us in many ways
And through our growing-up days
Father's Day cards are special too
Which one to choose that will do
Father's Day presents are masculine related
That are always greatly appreciated
For Fathers on Father's Day
Best wishes for a happy day

July Fourth

Celebrated on this day
Independence of the USA
Parades with floats and music too
Family gatherings, picnics and barbeques
The red, white and blue the colors of the day
Patriotic music to listen to and play
Naturalization ceremonies on this day
Welcoming new citizens in every way
Firework displays at night
Making the sky very bright

About Atmosphere Press

Atmosphere Press is an independent, full-service publisher for excellent books in all genres and for all audiences. Learn more about what we do at atmospherepress.com.

We encourage you to check out some of Atmosphere's latest releases, which are available at Amazon.com and via order from your local bookstore:

I Made A Place For You, poetry by Damian White

Melody in Exile, poetry by S. T. Brant

Covenant, poetry by Kate Carter

Near Scattered Praise Lies Our Substantial Endeavor, poetry by Ron Penoyer

Weightless, Woven Words, poetry by Umar Siddiqui

Journeying: Flying, Family, Foraging, poetry by Nicholas Ranson

Lexicon of the Body, poetry by DM Wallace

Loon Summer, poetry by Yvona Fast

Controlling Chaos, poetry by Michael Estabrook

Almost a Memoir, poetry by M.C. Rydel

Throwing the Bones, poetry by Caitlin Jackson

Like Fire and Ice, poetry by Eli

Sway, poetry by Tricia Johnson

A Patient Hunger, poetry by Skip Renker

Lies of an Indispensable Nation: Poems About the American Invasions of Iraq and Afghanistan, poetry by Lilvia Soto

The Carcass Undressed, poetry by Linda Eguiluz

Poems That Wrote Me, poetry by Karissa Whitson

Gnostic Triptych, poetry by Elder Gideon

About the Author

SUSAN MCLEOD resides with her husband John in Alplaus, New York. She is originally from Southold, Long Island, New York. In the fall of 1975, she moved to Troy, New York, attending Hudson Valley Community College's Nursing Program, and received her A.A.S. In 2007 she obtained a Bachelor of Arts from Russell Sage College in Troy, New York.

Susan made a career change from nursing to work in a nursing home Activities/Recreation department. Her favorite group activities were reading and writing poems with the residents. A collection of the residents' stories was placed in the lobby for everyone to read. She now volunteers in her community, enjoys outdoor activities, traveling, and pet-sitting for friends. An avid reader of historical/cowboy romance novels as well as poetry, she started writing her poems at fifty-one and continues to write today.

Website: www.susanpoetry.com

Facebook: Susan's Poetry

LinkedIn: Susan McLeod